Joy

Sasha Dugdale is a poet, translator
three collections of poetry with Ca
Red House. In 2017 she was awarde
2012 and 2017 she was editor of *Modern Poetry in Translation*. She is
co-director of the Winchester Poetry Festival.

also by Sasha Dugdale
from Carcanet Press

Notebook 2003
The Estate 2007
Red House 2011

Sasha Dugdale

CARCANET

for Paul

First published in Great Britain in 2017 by CARCANET PRESS Ltd,
Alliance House, Cross Street, Manchester M2 7AQ

Manufactured in England by SRP Ltd. A CIP catalogue record for this
book is available from the British Library, ISBN 9781784105044.

Contents

Joy

A dark stage. A woman in a rocking chair. Catherine Blake.

Silence.

They don't want me here... they don't want me...

An old woman, getting in their way,

                          under their feet.

Look what the cat brought in. An ancient orphan, no future to bless
her.

A sparrow, a spider, a nothing.

Good for nothing. And nothing will come of nothing... And nothing
will come of me now... A nothing left in darkness...

This is how it is. This is how it has been always. A parting.

We are parted

The fibres of our souls are spread. They cling –

A tear. A tear. And a tearing.

I am a rent shirt... I am a poor man's shirt and a pair of woollen
stockings and a patched jacket thrown from the hearse... Every
breeze shudders me... And no one wants me...

How I ache... How I ache... How I ache...

Nine days I laboured, nine days and nights I laboured, and on the tenth he gave me my freedom, singing. And my freedom was a wicker basket for the husks of shells. My freedom was a quilt of unspoken words...

looks around

A foreign kitchen, a winter light.

Seagulls very high in the clouds. How I ache.

A foreign hearth in London. My freedom is someone else's hearth in his town. The tenth day is drawing to a close. How I ache.

And he is gone, fled singing to some place I cannot reach. His angels came and he sang to them and they told him they needed him more than I did... Merciless, merciless angels... Merciless angels who know nothing of human despair. And he went with them. He nodded and spoke mild words and was soon gone... And he left a shadow of grime on his collar and a warm bed. And the angels had tall wings, like steeples, or like sails and spread white like the King's ship in dock, and they took him, only I couldn't see them, but I know how they looked, for hadn't he spent all his life in their company and mine? And didn't they sometimes appear in white like good children, and sometimes like ladies but barefoot, with rosy pink staining their necks and hands and ringlets in their hair? Their sighs were angel swords and their smiles were beams of light. He smiled at me, as if to say *can't you see how bonny they are today, on this, my deathday*, and there's the whole pity of it, for I couldn't see, and I never could.

8

And then the men took all his possessions and I could have sold the carpenter's glass and the copper and the pigments for I was wily like that but they said not to worry in my grief and they would provide for me although what was the providing to them when I eat like a bird and I can still keep house and they don't want me, they don't want me and they never will want me, no one will want me as he wanted me.

He wanted me. And his want is gone with him. And isn't that the ordinary way of things? When as a child I saw the widow ladies in their black bonnets following the coffins, didn't I laugh a little laugh to myself, because nothing so ordinary as a widowing could happen to me, armed with my black hair and black eyes. I walked out on my lover's walks in Battersea, where the wind from the river comes sweeping in and knocks the black bonnets and tears the handkerchiefs from their hands, those spider ladies creeping along behind their hearse. And I was the wind. The pitiless wind...

Laughs silently

I told him I pitied him! A lie. A lie to feast upon, because no man, no man in London could have pitied him. And he said he would love me

and it was as good as done then, my widowing

sealed to me.

I could have sewn a strip of black to my clothes every single day. Here... And here... and here... (*she clutches at her arms and her breasts*) and here... because he made my terrible widowing his life's business.

...Gone. Singing. Will I forgive him that singing... Singing like fruit breaking from its bud. And the bud's purpose gone!

He made me! He took me, soft and approximate as I was and blew the world into me. He put coals in my mouth and filled my hair with marble dust so I looked as white as one of his angels. But I was not his angel. I am rooted in the earth.

I'm angry.

I'm angry. My anger is an ache.

My lungs are full of howls, howls howling over each other.

What right did you have? You, you of all men, who let the slaves go free from the mill to run singing into the field, and the schoolboy! And the bonds and chains and taskmasters you dissolved into nothing....

And here I am! Your helpmate... your Kate... Bonded to nothing.

How I ache. How I ache.

Pause

These men who offer me charity for your sake, they honoured you and loved you. They took me for your maid when they first came and knocked on the door. And one of them took the bell pull to his mouth and kissed it. Funny young men! They honoured you and you swelled in the veneration, and I loved them then.

I hate them now, taunting me with their limbs and their eyes. They are more of your absence.

The more time they occupy the less you do.

Where are you? Where have you gone?

Husband!

Your death comes and counsels me.

It has a milky voice, it has a broken voice

it folds me in its pale arms and bids me

Think woman! Think of me.

I am suddenness.

I am the noise of cutting cloth so the remnant falls into a shivering heap.

I am colour in reverse and poetry backwards.

I pare away the ugly old past.

I seal every backwater with an iron till the tree of memory is a stump in you.

Put away that likeness in your head, old woman. It will cause more pain. Turn its face to the wall.

Think of me! Don't think of him.

Pause

How I ache. Oh how I ache

Pause

No. I say. No. Give me my despair.

I wish and feel and weep and while I weep I delight.

I remember everything.

Breathes deep

I remember how you taught me many things. When I met you a thousand years ago and that is not extravagant because you knew how to press on time and release it from its skin to grow you knew that about time and all manner of other wisdoms and how to release the sky from the indignant thistle, and colour from powder and line from copper and sense from letters which danced like demons on the page. And I refused to be tamed by you except in love. But one day I was scolding sweet Robert, your brother, and you said I should never see your face again unless I knelt on the floor and begged his forgiveness.

How hard it was then when I was still bent on winning the struggle though you told me later that I was fighting my own angel, couldn't I see it plain as daylight grappling with me and its heavenly face as pettish as mine

No I said in astonishment what angel, so you drew it for me on a scrap of paper as if we were a pillar and one creature, winged like a cup handle, and you locked me in your arms and said, look he is dissolving like salt and now we will struggle instead, but the struggle was a dance and we whirled about till the bottles rang on the shelves and laughed and laughed in exaltation.

So you freed me from the angel and you taught me what you knew so I should never bow to you I should be your equal in all practical matters and thenceforth you gave me a free hand to colour, and even draw which I willingly did. And I stitched and bound your books, and I cut the linen and polished the plates and made up inks and did all the work of an engraver at your side.

See my hands? Here. Look.

You said they were the hands of a craftsman.

Where to put them? (*She rubs her body with them*) They have never lain so long in my lap. They begin to gnaw at the air. (*She lays them palm up on her lap*) Two twisted vessels. All the craft trickles out of them...

All day they worked, these memory-hands. And he was beside me, working with his graver, or printing at the press. I don't remember once that he faltered, or considered how or what or why. He wrote and drew and painted as if something else painted through him and I coloured and sometimes drew as if he was drawing through me, and humility was in both of us, because we were instruments and equal in our apprenticeship.

Pause

No time for death. No. Death had no business nosing around. Caught you says death if you stand still. That's why children never catch their death, they are too quick for death, they slip past it, and if they don't then the angels come and release them. He called down to them innocent creatures and drew them little portraits on slips of paper

I wished for children.

I wished and wished. I patted their sprite heads and pulled them to me, their ghostly bodies, lifted them weightless into my lap and dandled their spirits. But God had put me on the earth for other things. God had put me on the earth to be an instrument and a companion.

And a lover.

I bore him no children, he was my child and I was his, and we were to each other brother and sister, parent and child, man and wife.

And when we made love we made love threefold. Across the generations and the sexes and the sacred prohibitions. And we made love as one.

I didn't know what love was. Nor did he. We were each other's pupils. And he sat brooding and looking and then threw himself down and wept that every shred of him was a harlot

but that I understood

I was wiser than he and I took his hand and told him

Between two moments bliss is ripe

He looked, his eyes shone how can this be sinful he cried

Generous love, how can we feel shame

there is no shame in this love, but only in self-love that envies

watching with its lamplike eyes the frozen marriage bed

but our narrow bed is warm and close

and two Gods dwell there, that's what he said.

Come and lie with me, Kate, come now to bed.

Pause

She shivers

Come now to bed.

Pause

My bed is empty. Where are you?

My bed is empty.

They have made me up a bed in a downstairs room because I cannot walk far and the bed is clean and white so I lie in it obediently knowing that it is to be my winding cloth

The old woman can't sleep

Give her valerian

The old woman can't sleep for remembering

Give her morphine

The old woman is a cold rock in black space

Give her back the sun

Pause

The walls are wordless. There is a clock ticking.

I have woken up from a dream of abundant colour and joy

I see his face and he is a shepherd and a piper and a god

I see him bent by the grate, setting the fire, and he is a fallen demon

I see him listening to the wind and sorrowing

I see wrath and misery, fire and desolation

A thousand fires in ancient London

And then the grass comes silent silent with the hardest colour of all

The mirth colour the corn colour the summer night colour

A thousand thousand summer nights pass

And children weave their daisy chains and place them on the heads of fallen idols

He wept he wept more tears than there were days

And never chained the door lest, he said, we drive an angel from it

And every morning he dipped his brush in wrath and mildness

And out of him tumbled the biggest things of all

All of them righter than the rightest calculation

And truer than any compass

Yet where they were right and true none could say

And how they were right and true none could guess

But I knew I knew

He was an eye, and the eye wept and frowned and smiled

The eye watched

The eye watered

The world was a mote in that eye

The mote was a world in that eye

And his brush was a blade and his tears made a lake.

How I ache how I ache

Pause

Sole partner and sole part of all these joyes he read to me in the
summer house where we sat when Mr Butts came knocking and
found us naked reading as we read every warm day the poor man
liked to tell that story to everyone as proof of the wildness of our life
though it never did seem wild to me but consistent in all respects and
full of holy sobriety which looks to the untrained eye like wild joy

William stood then and made a deep bow to Satan who had been
watching and said you are welcome to our garden sir Satan had a
round sad face like a waterwheel and seemed tired and full of pity,
he wore his rainbow snake around him and when he saw we meant
him no harm he bowed and shrivelled to a vapour

But Mr Butts came in and ate some grapes

Pause

Have no fear Satan, said William, we will not harm you

Yet all about us

war drifted from year to year like the seeds of weeds in autumn

and the looms made sails for warships, and the furnaces cast cannon
balls

men trained their horses to run towards death

all around us in schools and churches and meeting halls

corpses marched their filthy regular steps

and men spoke about it and the words themselves in pain, the words
thirsty

for new life, the words wanted mercy

and in the midst of all this a clearing in Lambeth and South
Molton Street and Fountain Court and a torrent of such wrathful
innocence pours forth, such light that violence staggered, violence
fell back

a spider a worm a beetle could approach it

but violence could not

an ant could find his children by it

but violence could not

And I tended that light

And he was the light

Pause

Who was I? And who was he?

I don't know!

Who was he?

I don't know!

Was he? Was he? The years passed in an eye-blink

They scrolled themselves up and were gone

The days are gone back to their creation

Was he? Or did I dream him?

Do these dreams make me who I am?

Who am I? Who am I?

A nothing left in darkness yet I am an identity

Terrible terrible

Pause

I have no strength in me

I am an old woman and she aches

How I ache

How I ache

The OLD WOMAN subsides, her head on her breast, for a few moments

What is this nothing beating at me?

I am —

Halts

I am —

Say it!

The shrivelled fruit that remains in the grass after the tree is felled

Remembrance but no inspiration

The cut flower which will not grow again in the grass

Remembrance

The ditch the stream has forsaken

But no inspiration

Frightened

I must dig deeper and deeper into my heart to find him, and it is no longer him

It is a story of him which will not serve I must bring him forth

And bring him forth for ever

Pause

His song in me. Is it my song?

Am I his song?

There was a song and he sung it but I sung it better

And a design which he taught me to see

And I saw it too

It was not a hard design, it was pale like flesh

It streamed in its hair and its limbs

Distorted in birth and death pang and horror

And quiet serene in the garden of affections

I looked across at him and he did not see me

He was talking then with the angel who had sat for Michelangelo and as I watched he nodded in understanding and that nod placed me then and there amongst the apostates I lay on the grass and the desert was all around me and even the devil would not come but my father the market gardener surveyed the land and called to me that even the desert would feed Battersea if enough dung could be brought from the city

I want to see!

Pray then.

But whenever I start a prayer which is one long thought burying
itself like a river in the porous mind until all that can be heard is
sacred underground water

whenever I start a prayer

I remember commissions and shopping and the new pumice and a
little twist of tobacco I bought for William and how the red pigment
is like blood and whether the neighbours will cease their fighting
and did I put out anything small for the cat that curls up on the worn
porch with its matted flea-ridden flank under the London sun

Pray!

The angel lifts up it was Gabriel says William but he is too busy to
hang around for long and the sky is bright with Gabriel rising over
the Thames like a firework

I want to see!

Pray then.

But my skull is as hard as a rock, there are no gates for prayers and
angels, and I am all jealous within

Well sing then, says William, or draw or come here to me and kiss me

So we draw, draw for hours and he draws me his emanation sulking
moth-like on an open flower moth-apostate moth-survivor

I want to see!

Pray.

Pause

I promise you will see, one day!

Ha!

I promise, Kate, and he put his arms around me and whispered hold fast to that which is good, and which of us is the angel now?

You, Kate, you are the angel.

Pause

We were of the devil's party.

Lustful, wrathful, naked.

The bird's airy senses the earthfulness of the worm

Truth! Wept over with the excess of joy

Truth! Never understood, only believed

I understood nothing (he chose me well)

From the beginning I believed and he breathed

Belief belief belief into me

And he gave my lungs air to breathe

Believe believe believe

I believed believed believed

But still I never saw.

Pause

Apart. From him

And our apartness was Moses

Peter, Paul and the hosts and hosts of angels

Dancing in our workshop, on the bed heads

Watching from the window seats and the door jambs

Dante, Milton, Shakespeare, grave as shillings and more frequent

And he met them as an equal

Fra Angelico Raphael

He welcomed them alone

Alone alone

He bowed to them

And still I never saw

And I breathed

Believe believe believe

Alone alone alone

Pause

I am choking.

Was I always alone?

Have I come to this?

Was it just him?

Pause

(*whispers, as if from a distance*) Kate, hold fast to me, Kate...

William! Where are you?

Stay Kate! Keep as you are! You have ever been an angel to me!

William!

Pause. The dark kitchen. The Old Woman.

(*whispers*) William...

The crow, the crow lets fall his love

But you are eagle and wren and dove

William...

Was I

Was I an angel?

Beloved Kate.

Weren't you listening to me?

Were you sorrowing and not listening?

William.

Listen now Kate

You will never be parted from me.

I hear you now, William. I see now...

I see

Darkness

The Widow and the Kaleidoscope

How mirrors can make an infinite pattern
of the randomly placed how one isosceles
glows with two crystals that slide even as
I watch there is no need to turn for even
the lightest movement will perturb
the pattern translates itself around the whole
in new perfections always perfect always
fearfully falling into new associations

The Ballad of Mabel

her eyes filled with tears again as she went on, 'I must be Mabel after all'

Mabel. Brown-eyed, unruly curls
She knows such a little!
An empty vessel, a swine amongst pearls
A stain from the inkbottle.

Her boots are old and the leather is worn
(The scuffs are just spat on)
Her dress is thin and her pinny torn,
And a sign round her neck reads: slattern.

She rubs her eyes with her fist till they're sore
And dozes with her cheek in a palm:
A sister that died, a father at war
Nights jigging babies to calm.

So many lessons to learn every night
She nurses, reads in the lull –
She must be a dunce, she can't get it right:
Dates just dance in her skull.

Mabel knows nothing, her house is poky
Her bed's as narrow as a coffin
And once she woke and her sister was choking
And the doctor – he couldn't do nothing.

Mabel's brother says he saw the Crimea
But came home for his chest
Once he told Mabel she had nothing to fear
And felt under her dress

Mabel knows nothing, nothing at all,
And her face is aflame
When she's cuffed by the teacher and turned to the wall
Her ears go pink with shame.

Mabel's hoop is at home, she says
She left her doll in bed
Mabel is standing alone – she says
She's playmates enough in her head.

Alice has a hoop and a man takes her boating
And her tea is ready on the table
Alice once had a dream she was floating
In tears, and feared she was Mabel.

The river is quiet, it's late and dusk
Mabel is wetting her toes
And watching the fish swallow her crust
In gold little O's.

She'll catch it, she thinks, if the splashes are heard
Or if she's seen –
But here she can lie in her spreading skirt
And dream her own dream.

Valentine's

I don't quite say it anymore, now the kids
Are teens and there are sudden wars, threads
Of conversations that no longer want to pass
Through the needle's eye of how we recast
Ourselves in new politics, new sadnesses, newspapers.
Irritability, like the substance left by vapours
That have long departed the alembic's lung
And taste with a quetsch's bitter tongue.
The hours and days mass themselves around
And harden like the filthy, frozen ground
On railway embankments on a mid-February day.
And that is in truth what I never quite say:
Those trashed slopes are home to the foxglove
An ancient restorer of the heart's beat, my love.

TONIGHT I thought of you. The rain was coming in from the west
But it was still dry and the spindle berries
Wound pink fruit into the harsh-cut hedge.
The animals were silent and still as pictures
And the moon was full and almost undressed –
Only a faint line of mist across the naked belly.

I walked on the hill and the darkness fell about me
Like heavy rain, and the leaves moved on the earth
Imitating mice and voles and butterflies.

It was blacker and blacker in the wood.
The chalk path led into such darkness
My heart almost failed me, but I kept going.

★

The span of a hand from thumb to furthest finger
Is a fraction of the span of a buzzard's wing
The buzzard's bristled neck is far stronger
Than the downy nape of a child sleeping
Which contains in its hollow a sweet cool
And softness as wild and small
As the green slope running down to a pool.
The eye is a poor organ in a poor head
It sees nothing in the evening but throws dark shapes
Into the shadows, it makes night in a deep wood.

DO YOU remember how we chanced upon a home
A long way from anywhere, with no way of arriving
Or departing, except by foot, as we had come?

We rested in meadow grass that was yellow and thriving
Breaking its way through the once level stone
Sharing its gains with the ragwort and ivy

The poppies and the briar rose.
Memory makes that devastation in our shape
A place of man that man forgoes

And leaves for memory to unmake
In wild creation that masks the hollow eye
And rotting hay and rusty rake

Nothing will ever die
That lives – though all its form be changed
So there we stopped a bit and lay

And now the hours and days are rearranged
The bodies lying there are beyond strange
Like angels glaring through one peacock eye.

Villanelle

When an ordinary man dies
Like that, all of a sudden,
There is no darkening of the skies,

Outside the lawns remain green and sodden
And vegetables pulled for supper lie
There is no sudden darkening of the sky

You can see the path his boots have trodden
The boots that slowly fold and subside
When an ordinary man dies

How ordinary! The cats still need feeding
The unbidden sun must endlessly rise
There is no sudden darkening of the skies

The shed is oven warm and full of flies
The beds grow and want weeding
When an ordinary man dies

It is a thing of great surprise
That no curtain is rent, no sacrifice lies bleeding
There is no sudden darkening of the skies

Only the ordinary parting with other lives
The barely audible tearing of ties
And no sudden darkening of the skies
When an ordinary man dies.

The Canoe

Two o'clock yesterday they put out.
The canoe was laden, we had seen to it,
With fishing nets, dried food, bread
And skins of water at their feet.
We walked into the sea, all of us
And the strongest gave them a shove
Swinging the boat like a battering ram
So it streaked, little goby, across the shallows
And we cheered, long and loud, bellowed
And hallooed, and some of us laughed
Real excited, mouths open, so the skies could see
Right down into our wet throats.

When did we stop cheering? The sea was calm
And they paddled fast, barely making a splash
Never looking back. We all stood silent
Some turned away when the colour of their clothing
Began to be the sea's colour, others when the motion of the paddle
Became the waves' motion, when there seemed only one figure
And then no figure in the boat, and then the boat too
Sank lower into the sea. And then you could only see
By shading your eyes and squinting, and then only in a telescope
And finally they slid out of the range of both eye and lens,
And the tiny smudge they had become remained on the horizon
Long after they had disappeared, and we all knew it was a trick of
                                                      the light.

Several days that week we gathered in groups at the sea's edge
And one morning I went down in a thick sea mist
Not to look – there was nothing to see except the white fog

And the white sun which reflected itself in every droplet –
But to consider the absence of stars and sky and sea
And as I walked into the shallows and looked down
I could see quite clearly the clouds of tiny fish
Each no bigger than a needle, bright-eyed, hair-boned
Exploding in shoals of sand as I placed each foot.
Moving like a giant away from the invisible shore
And into a claustrophobia of white, blinding and dank
I thought of the canoe, a hundred and twenty miles away by now.

Once they had turned their backs on home it was gone
They could have changed their minds no more
Than time can turn its face to the morning star
Their paddles might have been clock hands –
Sixty small splashes every minute, sixty times an hour
Their will kept time, and if they did not conquer time
Then they moved at its pace, they were time's ghosts.
They never once looked back, and watching them leave
I supposed we were the past, we stood stock-still
And gradually slipped backwards, out of sight and mind
And turned away from the shore in dribs and drabs
And resumed our thin lives beyond the highest tides.

Only a handful of days after the canoe fell from sight
I heard a song I thought had left our soil with them
The singer had gone, the song remained:
Whistled hesitantly, then with more confidence
And then sung, the notes slightly changed
All sorts of subtle variations, ornaments
Where there had been none, an act of memory
To begin with, then clawed over, gnawed upon,
The singer slept on the mess of words

And they grew through his dreams, snatched
At his heart, shot bare roots through his memory
The words shocked me when I heard them then:

On the night we parted the sky was black with tears
It was once white with stars, I am sure of this
Or I was sure until I heard it, as it came twisting
In the air with its dark hurting sound, set free
From the mouth to rampage its mourning through the trees –
Even before I heard it, the black sky was in my head
The tears in my eyes, this was only the whistling proclamation
Of the new, as it set about the past like a wild god
Like a forest fire. All I have now are the stumps
Of memory and the waste, and as the new growth
Comes I rejoice – I won't live to see the trees grown.
White with stars, only a chink now, it was always black I think.

For days and weeks their homes were left, their possessions
Lay untouched, but then the shameless went into their rooms
And took, and the pious went into to feast on the bones
And with higher reasons took their share, and the zealots wept.
But every day their number grew fewer, red-faced or brazen
They'd tread the paths with cases and boxes and chests
And some wanted souvenirs: combs, bracelets, baubles
To remember by, the memory a most hungry organ
Forced men in and in again, under carpets, floorboards
No end to the lengths they'd go for a memento's sake.
They could not bear a thing dispossessed, a thing un-useful.
The spare goods made them chafe and grieve, from there to thieve.

Still, an insult to us to watch homes decay, their insult
Thrown casually back at us, the ones left behind

To be occupied and overcome by ivy and dust and mould.
The knives rust in spots, and the spots increase like forget-me-nots
Scattering the blade's length. The books moisten and their paper
                                                              hastens
To wholeness, their words unspeak themselves in tree pulp.
But it is the food that is eaten first, it gives up its spore and eggs
Sags and tumbles into itself and is crowned triumphant by tiny flies,
Bait for the spiders who build boats of silk with such reverence
Such regularity of movement I think of the canoe when I watch them.
This insult is paid meticulously, gram by gram, beat by beat
In skeins of neglect and flowering distress.

So who can blame the ones who broke in and stole
Who brought on the collapse, by breaking in doors and windows
Who fell about in a wild frenzy then, and drove at ceilings, boards
With hooked poles, hoping for treasures to come pouring forth.
Then, encouraged by the fierce and glorious joy of destruction
They cudgelled chairs with chair legs, tossed cups like coconuts
Stamped and urinated and spat at the walls in spasms
Of horror *glad to see the back of you fucker* and *pay back time*
And when all was done and broke: *you never coming back
Stranger*. No one admits to these outpourings, even if caught
Crouching, defecating on a bright rug. They are surprised as dogs
Shit trembling out of them, struggling to adjust.

Who set the hovels alight one evening? It was a mercy killing.
Flames, the blackness of incinerated wood cleans us all
Of signs. I want no museums to them, I want no reimaginings.
I can't remember them I don't know who they were
Or why they went. History is a black night and only fools
Think they can escape its oncoming: it comes from the sea
It struggles out of the water like the great runt and rubs its hands

Over the tides. It takes today's lineaments and wrings them –
Wrongs them, spreads them to shrink and pale, then trades
In the cast-offs, makes a busy market maligning and misaligning
What did fit the day and its people like their own skin –
It finds crowns for shrunken heads and garments for naked greed.

In the room two children together, but one is sick and shivering
She lies and breathes and feels hot and cold. The other is singing.
I can conjure up the day of their leaving, I see their backs moving
Their shoulders under their shirts rising and falling, the paddles
                                                              lifting
Distance makes the movement meaningless, a repeated shrugging
As if amazed but indifferent; a white flower sprouting in the sea
On either hand, repeatedly. But were they ours, says the sick child
And I say: I must have been a child myself when they left
I don't know who they were anymore, and whose they are now
No one knows. Are you sad? She says with dry lips
I cry all the time. I look at the sea and I cry.
I cry because they are gone and the sea is empty.

The years pass. They pass in long procession like prophets
Never looking our way, never allowing themselves to be known.
I have spent such a time on the beach the fish think I am a friend
They clamour around my ankles, swim to where water and sand meet
To where the shallows cannot possibly allow them to exist.
I worry about them, shoo them, scold them out to sea
Storms sixty miles away light up the darkening sky
Drops of rain fall on the sea and the land alike
What is it like to look back at this land from out there?
The clouds tripping on it and upsetting their load
A black line. A line which comes into focus and then vanishes again:
A possibility a certainty a fact a possibility a nothing

Cutting Apples

This morning I sat and cut apples.
I cut them into four, and then I nicked each part
And brought my knife around the curve.

And through long practice I kept my thumb
Up tight against the blade, and when I twisted
The blade inside each quarter it returned to my thumb.

And the quarters I put into the pan with lemon
And the peel and corners of apples I heaped on the board.
There was a silence. My thoughts wandered.

I thought about absence, which so hates to be considered
It throws the thoughts back out like thieves
And bolts the door behind them.

More and more my thoughts besieged his hovel
Tarred wooden shelter on the beach,
Again and again the thoughts came limping

Black-eyed, dented, tossed by the inhospitable
Absence, back to me at my cutting board
To be dispatched again with an oath

I want to know, says the despot mind
What this place is, what is inside the home
Of absence? Where are my best men?

I sent my best thoughts, the ones I keep
To guard me through the dark hours
They too came reeling and bloodied back

At last my youngest thought came to me
Father says he, let me try, where others failed
Let me enter the house of absence

Whatever knowledge it might contain
I will fight for it and bring it home
And off he flew, my most recent thought

Who came to the home of absence
And found the door wide open
Swinging like a thumb on a knife blade

He fell in love with absence
And threatens now to return forever
He is betrothed and thinks of nothing else

Ironing the Spider

My most violent act: once ironing a spider.
She had climbed between sheets on the ironing board
And was resting in the pastel scent of laundry:
A large spider, slightly prim, self-assured.

I can't abide violence. I can't even swat a fly.
The death of this meaty widow left a creeping stain
And a horror in my throat, like the first kill
Like the first time you cause another creature pain.

I gagged. Only a little, and momentarily,
Unable to regain the balance that had been undone
By introducing death to this pink-white refuge:
Violent, unpleasant death by branding iron.

I have since seen her soul all scorched and resentful
Her spirit crushed and oozing. I am reminded then
Of the railway victims on the Pskov station board.
It read: do you recognise these men?

Part-covered by a red flag. Maimed by trains
As they staggered home, chased
Silently from behind, a horrid shove
Removing the drunken smile from their face.

I knew them all. We were of the same species
Not *sapiens* perhaps, but *homo* for sure
I could have ironed their shirts, their sheets,
Sat waiting for them, cross-legged on the kitchen floor.

The Ballad of the Sewing Kit

A little packet of needles, wrapped in a paper sheath
Found in the empty drawer of a bedside table
With *for your convenience* embossed on the leaf
And *Imperial Hotel* emblazoned on the label.

Meant for loose stitching, buttons, holes in heels
In the imperial past of make-do-and-mend
Where every second shop was bobbins and reels
And no useful object's life ever came to an end.

I've long forgotten what empire was my host
Or even how the hotel looked, the room and the bed
I only remember that I was lost
And I pocketed the packet and the tiny spool of thread.

Then years. And then darning children's tights
I came across the whole minute sewing kit
How grandly imperial for a thing so very slight
Full of airs like the darning needle lying in the shit

And I could see all of a sudden the room, the bed:
The breeze was hot, the open windows clattered
The walls were green and bare, and overhead
A white fan lisped and fluttered.

It was August, hated month, and the pregnant air
Coupled with the city and blew from her cheeks
Tobacco, soured milk, soiled underwear
I stood on the balcony and breathed in deep.

Out there a thousand women stitched a thousand patches
Drawing the thread through and through again
They looked from up here like a thousand lit matches
Or a thousand lamps burning one steady flame.

For all of them a single finger and a single thumb
A buttoned overall, a hook for the coat
And one shameful sight: the kitchen in a slum
I once glimpsed as the door closed.

Where was I going, what business had I there?
August and the winds dog the earth's heel.
Three needles and some buttons to keep as spare
A tiny safety pin, and a black cotton reel.

Pfingsten in Paterki

Tanned faces, frowning in the sun:
a group of girls filmed in headscarves
by an enemy combatant.
You should hate me, he says,
I could kill your menfolk, your boyfriends
and yet you let me take your photograph.
He took it back to his atelier
and hung it in the developing room.

I like their dresses. I like the red and the composition:
sprigged, floral. I like their sincerity
I like the fact they are alive in Kaluga,
flames of spirit, talking like teenagers
in 1943. I like the fact that there were hot days
when the wind came rushing down the dusty road
and a German soldier, holding a Voigtländer
could still speak in tongues.

(*Pfingsten*: Pentecost in German)

How my friend went to look for her roots

It took several trains, a bus ride
along wide roads through a ploughed desert
past empty bus stops many miles apart
to arrive at dusk in a small town.
First wooden houses, the gardens full of cabbages
then grey blocks, the swinging telegraph wire,
unlit bicycles, the damp earth and its suffocating vapours.

This little town had an ancient centre, but nowhere to eat. The
little hotel was shut for repairs a thousand years
in the completing, and the woman who poked her head from a
window said:

– If you're from here then why don't you stay with your family?

– My family left.

So, asked the woman, why come here then? Which, thought my
friend, was a reasonable question, as the darkness came hard across
the open land and up the street and nowhere to sleep that night
except an empty room where the builders kept their tools
on a pallet and under a thin blanket.
She slept hardly at all that night, for fear of falling off the mattress,
she rued her purpose and scratched her skin
and vowed she would leave at dawn if she had to walk.

Dawn arrived, the pink sky was vaster than anywhere she'd known.
Geography is a strange thing, this town left beyond
the known world, the comfortable road, on the edge of nothing,

from where her family had been plucked
with a million others, carrying only memories of home

walking, walking out of the town.

Mappa Mundi

I know where the white violets grow
                By some unravelling rolls of roof felt
And the orchids, come May,
                I know which slopes they scatter.
I know the field for peewits
                When it's waterlogged and black
And the best, most heady smell
                Of silage, I know where to breathe in.
I know where spindle berries light
                A fence for bryony and a hedge for sloes
The best tracks on a muddy day
                The smell of wet, the badger lurching across
A glow worm, a buzzard, a lark
                The inland egret, the horse.

There's a den in the copse
                A dead mole, a man with a wound on his face
I know the walk he takes
                The way he clutches his buttock
Another who takes a hockey mask
                To the woods, and wears white gloves.
I know where there are fridges
                Mattresses, old cars and oil cans
And sour tight berries
                Apples and damsons fall ungathered.
How far the dog walkers
                The mothers and toddlers, Sunday ramblers
Their routes, their returns
                I know them all.

The splitting of hair-like streams
                        Names that become accepted
Names that fade like old shops
                        New fences, new asphalt and verges
New signposts, old paths, sudden hills
                        Disappointing smallnesses, surprising drops
Hidden meadows, green waters
                        Holy places, at least to me.
Is the world not like this?
                        An invented place of moving and belonging
A delicious hatred of the other place
                        A sorry love of this one
Bacterial growth along roads
                        Light caught like a thing unwanted in a tree.

Kittiwake

Your jizz, little gull, is the traveller's
jizz, the wanderer, who sees the black, flecked ocean
barren like the steppe, and drops to feel the cut of its
rough coat, sail boat-like in the dizzying swell
and lift again, casual as the inhabitant of a planet poisonous to man.
No doubt you might have hung around
but all the accommodation offered to you was the white tenement
blasted with guano, crumbling with the chalk's sickness
the clamour of children from the playground in the yard.
Those wings, tipped with ink, as if you had signed the dotted line
With one, signed up to country and nation and place –
          then in an instant turned mid-air
                              and dipped the other wing in the bottle
to run your signature through. Not citizen! Not patriot! Not I –
from now on the expanse and the blackness will be my place,
amongst you I will make no home, only a perch
as fishermen perched on the edge of a hostile continent,
so the kittiwake will perch, briefly, all the better to fear
You – the inland, the citizen.

Days

On Svetlana Aleksievich's book on women's experiences in the Second World War, 'The Unwomanly Face of War'

1

When all is said and done, the worst that has happened
is only this: crawling in a ditch, naked, except for an old dress
ripped throat to groin and stained with blood.
Is this the worst the fates can cut out
for me with their long shears? I am not ashes
I have my wits. I have the shadows of memories
grand pianos, cinemas, milk bluing in a storm
a man losing his child to a king who rode him down
silently, on a road like this: long and unmetalled
with the waymarkers snapped at their hilts
the milestones toppled and disfigured.
I had a future, and remember it well,
how it was always there, like the promise of light
at the edge of the curtain.

2

it was only the nurses who made us feel shame
if they had come to know of it
they would have made us feel ashamed
we did not want them to know about it
we knew they would make us ashamed
if they had come to know about it
only the nurses could do that

3

On Thursday I drove out of the city.
The land was old and barely alive
It gave me the geometric shock
When life unroots itself
And the rearview mirror shows
A woman on the horizon of a hole
Living, but incinerated.

She spoke, and it was not for a while
I knew it was me speaking.
She was practising what to do
If someone has a stroke,
If someone has a memory loss
Or his heart stops beating

4

War is liquid-thought-fire
it burns the mind –
I feel you are burnt irretrievably
your imagination exposes beams
your memories are shapeless ruins.

I've been scalded. As when I pick the pan up wrong
or let the steam hiss out over my hands.

I heard of men in steamboats
when the boiler blows
tripe-men, who stand a few minutes
whole but boiled.

5

The interpreter shows me a dusty parlour
And hands me a broom.
No one is as tidy as me, I pant
I get every little mote of dust into the pan
I use spit instead of water
This place will fucking shine.

But the dust falls and falls
Because every action
Has an equal and opposite
And my skin is wearing through
Shedding particles
Like white soot
On the mantelpiece.

6

I could so easily give up my house
I've made a list of what to take:
Notebooks, phone and plug, handcream
A thermos, knife, warm clothes.
But it makes me anxious
That I will start to smell after twenty-four hours.

7

My daughter does my hair in two pigtails
I like her holding it and twisting it up
I remember someone else putting it up
When I was a child.

I remember how she brushed it.
Me, in a hospital bed with a beaker.
I remember how she combed it
Carefully. Me in the parlour
With the candles lighting my way.

8

I have no right to grief
I am whole
I have no right to grief
I am whole
I have no right to grief
I am whole

9

My wife was a stenographer
She typed the word rape
Forty times in one hour
She sat in a bank of women
Making records of what had been done
And she felt herself to be lucky
To be alive and unscathed.
My wife lost only a few near relatives
And a first husband
And she had a stillbirth
Whose name she wrote in water.

10

Their flag was a tablecloth from a basement
With marks where they stubbed out their cigarettes
And soup stains and rings where they set their glasses.
Not everyone died fighting.
Some, like my own,
Died when he fell into a river.
He was drunk. He'd come looking for a coin
We never gave him one.
He said bitches.
He left staggering.

11

I can't help wanting sex
So near to death – I mean
Geographically. A mere two thousand miles
And the odds on survival drop
Like the mercury drops in me
At some chance word or gesture,
Your face, your look.
I want perfection
But every day the people pass
They have walked for miles
And each of them takes something
Small and dark from our closed garden.
I fear they are taking days.

12

You called me 'child'
It was a play-act since
I was wiser than the sea
But after you came home
You stopped, in respect
To the damage done
And called me only
mother.

The Daughter of a Widow

From my birth I had heard those words
As a small child I saw them from her lips

And learnt them myself. 'Killed in the war'
But having known no absence they were shapely

Trailing, veil-thin, through the glass and grit
Which had by then permeated through alveoli

Entered the bloodstream, lodged in the fingertips.
No one may know that which is death

Before their time, and I saw only that
Which is elderly before its time, disappointment.

She had no more knowledge than I, how he
Was hit, by whom, and was he thinking of her

Like that mortally wounded man who, smiling, asked the nurse
To open her gown and show him her breasts

Because he had not seen his wife for nearly a year.
Unhappy woman, she rushed from his bed as he reached

And only returned when he was dead
She remembers, old now, thinking always of the breach,

How the same smile stretched his lips in death.

For Edward Thomas

Not a cloud in the sky and the pier hangs in mist
No swiftness and not a cloud to mark this soul
But brightness all around so fiercely torpid
Nothing can be seen at all.

The front is so wide I walk with my eyes closed
And the sea breathes shallow as a roosting dove
My unblemished soul goes shapeless through the light:
Pale calf-hide, it has need of the cloud's love.

There you stand, like the fish upon its tail,
Who tasted all the various hells upon the earth
And was marked for ever by the passage of a cloud
And the rain, and the birds, and all such things of worth.

Acknowledgements

Poems in *Joy* have been previously published in *Poems in the Waiting Room* in Hampshire NHS Trust, *PN Review*, *Edinburgh Review*, *The Rialto*, *The Irish Times*, *Agenda*, and *New Walk*. 'Kittiwake' was first published in *Birdbook: Saltwater and Shore* (Sidekick Books, 2015) and 'The Ballad of Mabel' was commissioned and first published by the *Alice: Ekphrasis at the British Library* project. 'Days' was first published in *The Long White Thread of Words: Poems for John Berger* (Smokestack, 2016).